Greenhaven World History Program

GENERAL EDITORS

Malcolm Yapp
Margaret Killingray
Edmund O'Connor

Cover design by Gary Rees

ISBN 0-89908-113-4 Paper Edition
ISBN 0-89908-138-X Library Edition

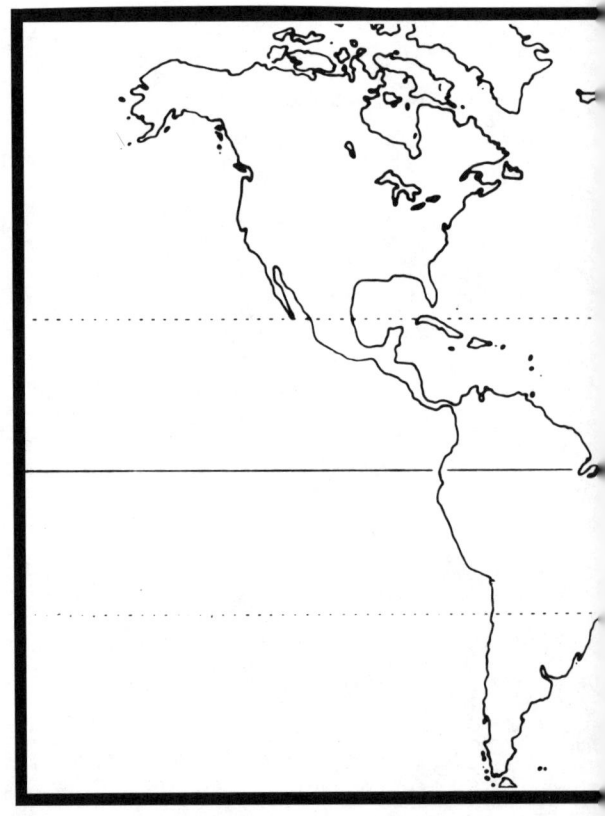

© Copyright 1980 by Greenhaven Press, Inc.

First published in Great Britain 1975 by
GEORGE G. HARRAP & CO. LTD
© George G. Harrap & Co. Ltd. 1975

All rights reserved. No part of this publication may be reproduced in any form or by any means without the prior permission of Greenhaven Press, Inc.

THE RUSSIAN REVOLUTION

by David Killingray

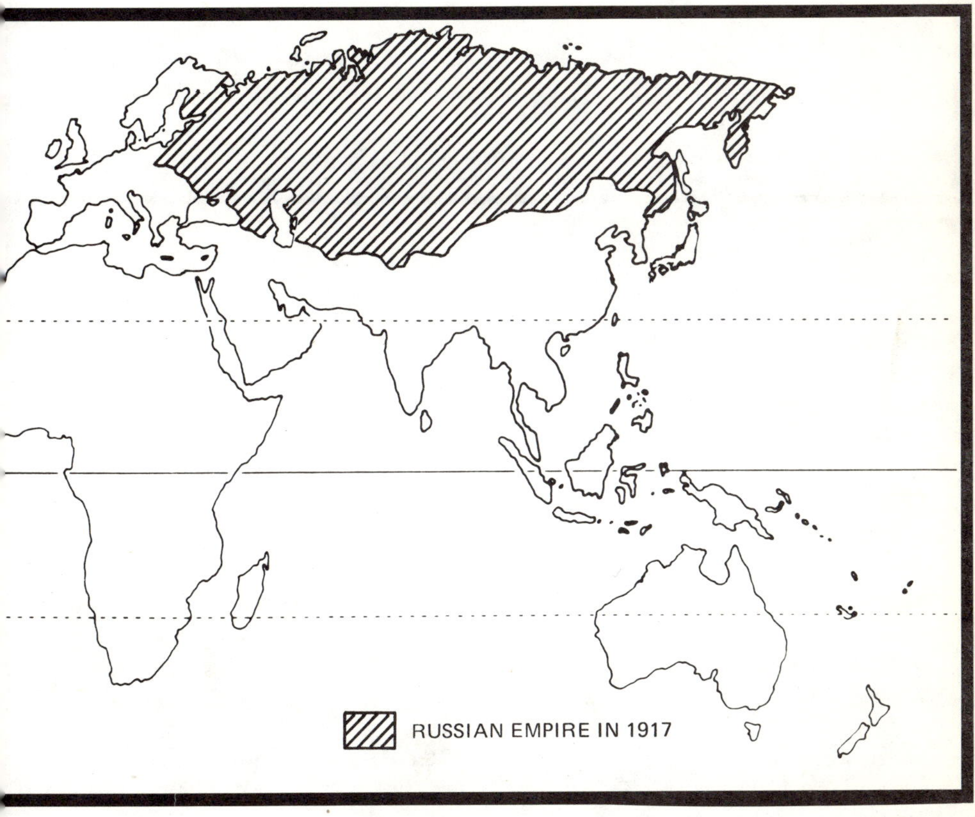

RUSSIAN EMPIRE IN 1917

Greenhaven Press, Inc.
577 SHOREVIEW PARK ROAD
ST. PAUL, MN 55112

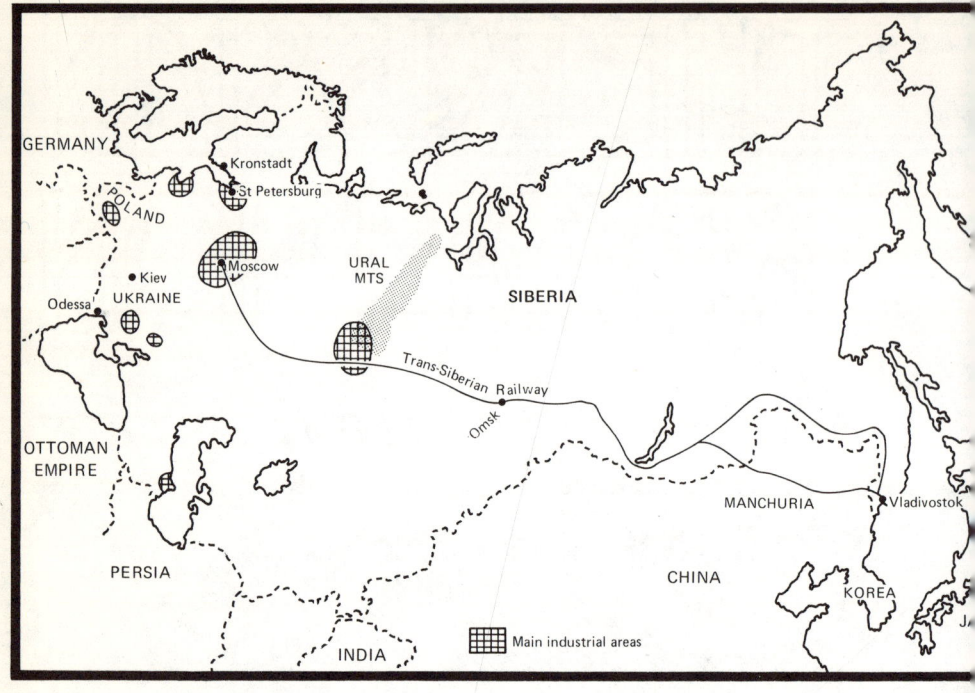

The Russian Empire, 1917

Russia in the late nineteenth century was the largest country in the world. Her territory stretched from Europe across central Asia and Siberia to the Pacific Ocean. Most of the Asian lands had been conquered by Russia between the seventeenth and nineteenth centuries. Only about half of the 130 million people in this vast empire were Russians. The others belonged to many nationalities who spoke different languages. There were Poles, Finns, Ukrainians, Uzbeks, and Tatars. Some belonged to the Russian Orthodox Church, the state church, but many were Roman Catholics, Muslims, or Buddhists. Many of these national groups wished to be free of Russian control.

PEASANT RUSSIA

Although Russia had an enormous army and appeared to be one of the most powerful states in the world, she suffered from several weaknesses. Compared to industrial countries such as Britain and Germany, Russia was economically backward. Her modern industries were begun later than those of Western Europe whom she lagged behind.

Russia was still mainly an agricultural country. Ninety per cent of the people were peasants. They lived in the countryside and either farmed small plots of land or worked on the large wheat estates of the south. Until the 1860s most peasants had been serfs. This had meant that they worked for a landowner and were not allowed to leave their village. At that time few peasants owned the land on which they worked. Most land was owned by the State, the Church, and a small number of nobles and businessmen. When the serfs were freed in 1861 some did buy land and become prosperous. But most peasants became poorer. The population was increasing rapidly and there was not enough land to go round. (D1)* Many peasants became landless labourers or went to work in the new industries which were being built in the countryside, and in the growing towns.

NEW INDUSTRIES

In the middle of the nineteenth century Russia began to develop new industries. A large part of the equipment and money needed for building factories, mines and railways came from the industrial countries of Western Europe. This meant that many Russian industries were foreign owned. Russia paid for the equipment and money with exports of grain and timber and with taxes taken from the peasants. Many of the new industries were in cities such as Moscow and St Petersburg (it was called Petrograd after 1914; it is now Leningrad). The workers lived in sprawling slums and worked long hours in bad conditions for low wages. Russia's factories were among the largest in the world. Thousands of men and women worked in the same factory buildings. These were ideal places for agitators to organize trade

Famine in a village of the Volga region, 1892. Peasants being fed by a charity organization. Famine was common in the countryside and led to riots

*The reference (D) indicates the numbered documents at the end of this book.

Working men with wooden spoons eating from a common bowl. A picture drawn in St Petersburg 1905.

unions and plan revolution.

At the head of the Russian Government was the Tsar, Nicholas II (reigned 1894-1917). He was an absolute ruler. That means that he could appoint anyone he liked to be a member of the Government. Not a clever man, he was ill-suited to run a country as big and important as Russia. Nicholas believed that he had been appointed by God to rule. He didn't want an elected Parliament to help him govern or to advise about new laws. Most of the nobles, officials and church leaders who helped to run the slow, badly organized system of government agreed with this. And those who opposed the Government or tried to bring about changes were either imprisoned or sent into exile.

Tsar Nicholas II with his only son Alexius

THE REVOLUTIONARIES

During the late nineteenth century many Russians, especially the younger and more educated people, wanted to solve their country's problems of poverty and harsh government. Some of the wealthier people, such as lawyers and businessmen, hoped that changes would come peacefully. Others thought that conditions were so bad that gradual reform would not work. Only a revolution could change Russia.

Many different ways of starting a revolution were tried. Some revolutionaries favoured the murder of important politicians and officials. Others thought it was more important to stir up the peasants against their landlords. But these methods did not work.

Some of the revolutionaries were followers of Karl Marx (1818-83). Marx was a German thinker who wrote about the social and economic conditions of Europe in the nineteenth century. He thought that industrial countries like Britain and Germany would go on growing in power and wealth. The powerful owners (capitalists) of the industries, who also ruled these countries, would become richer while the workers who made the goods in the factories would become poorer. He was sure that eventually there would be a revolution in which the working class would take over the factories and the running of the Government. (D2) All industry would then be owned by the people who would share out the riches of the state equally to everybody in the country. Marx

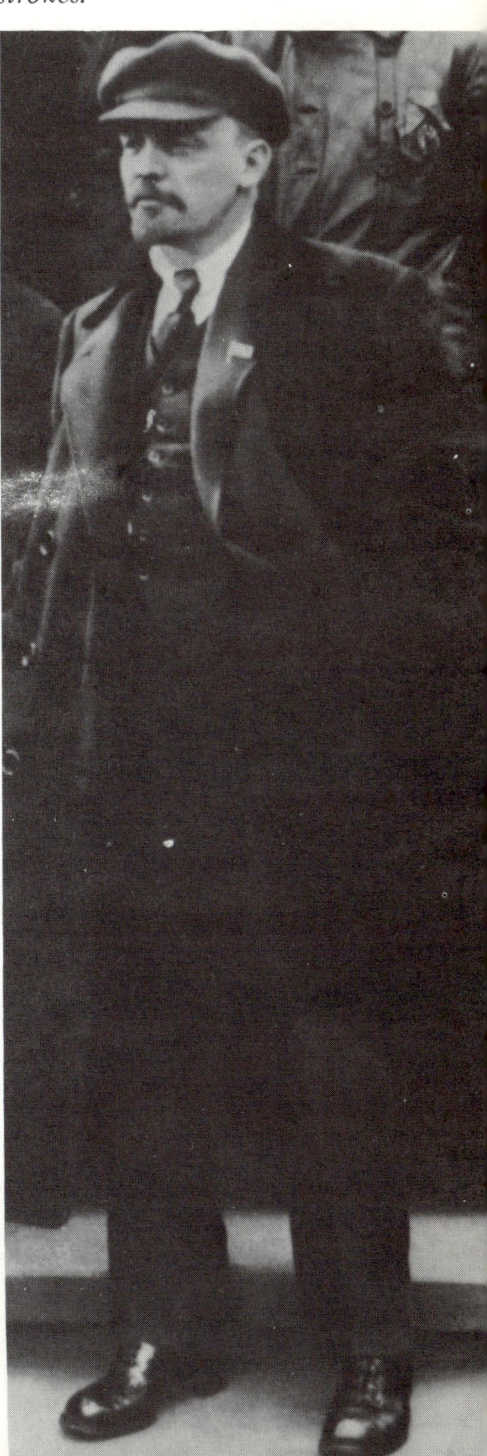

Lenin. A photograph taken in 1919 at a May Day rally in Red Square, Moscow. Lenin died in 1924 at the age of 54 after several strokes.

thought that this socialist revolution was bound to happen because it was a law of history (like a scientific law). He believed that the revolution would first start in Britain and Germany because they were the most advanced industrial countries with more factory workers, although later he thought that it might start in Russia.

One of the people most strongly influenced by Marx's writings was Vladimir Ilyich Ulyanov, known as Lenin. Lenin was born in 1870, the son of a schoolmaster. His elder brother, Alexander, was executed for attempting to kill Tsar Alexander III in 1887. This had a great effect upon the young Lenin. He studied law at university but was expelled for taking part in anti-government riots. In the 1890s he was imprisoned and sent to Siberia for his political activities. Lenin and others developed what Marx had written into the ideas that we now know as Communism. Lenin did not believe in waiting for the revolution to happen. His aim was to use every possible means to start a revolt in Russia. He therefore organized a group of Marxists called Bolsheviks into a disciplined band of trained revolutionaries. (D3) He insisted that his ideas should be accepted. This did not make him very popular with other revolutionaries. But Lenin was clever and very determined. He did not care what other people thought. He was sure that he was right and that revolution would come in Russia.

The Tsarist Government was well aware of these revolutionaries and their activities. Members of the various groups were often caught and put in prison. Lenin himself spent many years in exile in Britain and Switzerland.

THE RUSSO-JAPANESE WAR

In 1904 Russia went to war with Japan over who should dominate Korea and Manchuria. (*Japan's Modernization*)* Japan won and Russia and the Tsar were in trouble. The troubles were not so much because of what had been lost in the war but because of the shame of defeat. For Russia had been beating Asian countries for four hundred years: now one of these despised Asian countries had beaten her. The Government's failure in the war and the terrible

*Titles in brackets refer to other booklets in the Program

The Russo-Japanese war. Russian soldiers preparing to defend an advanced post in Manchuria 1904

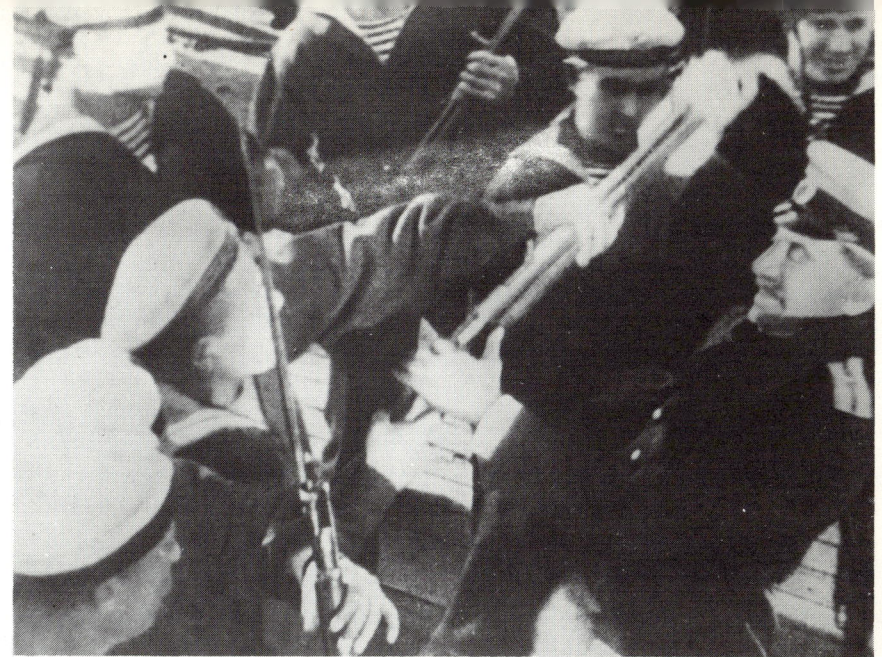

Sailors of the Black Sea fleet mutiny during the revolution of 1905. This picture is a recreation in the Soviet film Battleship Potemkin *made by Sergei Eisenstein in 1925*

living conditions of the people led to peasant riots and strikes throughout Russia.

THE REVOLUTION OF 1905

On 'Bloody Sunday', 9th January 1905, troops opened fire on a workers' demonstration in St Petersburg. (D4,5) Throughout the spring and summer there were strikes in the towns, riots in the countryside and assassinations everywhere. In June the crew of the battleship *Potemkin* mutinied, took over their ship and sailed along the coast of the Black Sea, bombarding towns on the shore. In October the nation was paralysed by a general strike which lasted for ten days.

The Tsar at last agreed to make important changes in the Government. He issued an 'October Manifesto' which promised to establish a Parliament, or Duma. (D6) The Duma was to be elected by some of the people but it could

The State Duma in session 1906. A portrait of the Tsar hangs above the head of the president of the Duma

Peter Stolypin, prime minister of Russia 1906-11. He ruthlessly suppressed all attempts at revolution

only give advice to the Tsar about how the country should be governed. This made little difference to ordinary people in Russia.

The revolution of 1905 failed for several reasons. By agreeing to a Duma the Tsar's Government gained the support of many of the better-off people who were content with gradual reforms. There were other people who wanted more rapid reforms and who were dissatisfied with the plan for the Duma. They wanted a Parliament, similar to those in France and Britain, which was elected by most of the people and which would be responsible for governing the country. Thus the opposition to the Tsar's government was divided. Also many people who supported reform were frightened by the revolutionary violence and wanted law and order restored. The revolutionaries who hoped to change the whole way of life in Russia were few in number and the workers could not afford to remain on strike. But most important were the army and police who stayed loyal to the Government and helped to put down revolts in the towns and the countryside.

The Tsar still ruled Russia. He could ignore the Duma or just close it down if he did not like what it said. Nicholas was helped by a very able minister, Peter Stolypin. He persuaded the Tsar to introduce reforms in agriculture and education which would make some of the peasants more prosperous. He hoped these richer peasants would want peace in the countryside and thus help to prevent revolution. Above all Stolypin wanted to develop the wealth of the vast area of Siberia and thought that many of the problems of crowded European Russia could be solved if men emigrated to the new lands.

For a few years peace and prosperity seemed to be returning to Russia. But it was only a breathing space. Stolypin was shot dead in 1911. During the next few years there were renewed outbreaks of strikes and rioting. When war with Germany broke out in 1914 Nicholas hoped that it would unite the nation in support

Russian troops stop for food on their way to the front line during the First World War, April 1915

of him and his Government. Some of his ministers feared that war would only bring revolution. Lenin was sure of this. He realized that Russia was unlikely to stand the strain of a long war. (*The Two World Wars*)

THE FIRST WORLD WAR

For Russia the war was an almost total disaster. In the first two and a half years the army suffered more than five million casualties. In many parts of the front line the troops were reduced to fighting with their bare hands because the whole transport system had broken down and it was impossible to keep them properly supplied with food and weapons. The situation was no better behind the lines. In the big cities the breakdown of the transport system meant shortages of food and fuel and so led to strikes and riots. (D7)

When Nicholas decided to take personal command of the troops at the front he handed over the running of the Government to his wife, the Tsarina. She was completely under the influence of a religious teacher, Rasputin. When any of the Tsar's ministers tried to say anything against him, Rasputin persuaded the Tsarina to dismiss them. The Government of Russia was therefore paralysed as one incompetent minister was

Demonstration in front of the Winter Palace, Petrograd 1917

succeeded by another in rapid succession. In the last twelve months of Nicholas's rule there were no less than four Prime Ministers, three Foreign Ministers and three War Ministers.

The Russian people had supported the war with enthusiasm at first. But by 1917 the peasants and workers had become heartily sick of it. Millions of men had been forced to join the army. Food production fell and prices rose. The corruption and weakness of the Government became more and more obvious every day. Many Russians wanted a strong Government that would fight the war properly. (D8) Even some of the nobles and officials who supported the idea of absolute rule began to plan how to get rid of Nicholas. Russia was on the verge of breakdown. This was an ideal situation for the revolutionaries who wanted to overthrow the Government.

THE FEBRUARY REVOLUTION

In late February 1917 strikes and food riots broke out in Petrograd. (D9) The soldiers called out by the Government to restore order mutinied (D10) and joined the rioters. Tsar Nicholas ordered the Duma to dismiss but its members set themselves up as the Provisional Government of Russia. On the next day Nicholas abdicated. (D11)

During the next six months the Provisional Government tried to govern Russia. Its leaders were reformers and moderate revolutionaries. They wanted to do two main things: win the war against Germany, and hold elections for a new Duma which would then decide what changes had to be made in Russia. But the Provisional Government was not strong enough to rule. It did not have enough power. Throughout Russia factory workers, peasants and soldiers had organized themselves in to councils, or soviets, which held local control. One of the strongest soviets was in the capital, Petrograd. It was well organized and supported by so many workers and soldiers that it could act as another government alongside the Provisional Government. In the countryside law and order broke down and peasants seized the land for themselves. (D12) At the 'front' thousands of soldiers, most of whom were peasants, deserted and went home. And many of the national groups set up governments independent of Russia.

When the February revolution broke out Lenin was living in Switzerland. He was against the policies of the Provisional Government and wanted to return to Petrograd to organize the Bolsheviks ready to seize power. The Germans, eager to see revolt and chaos weaken Russia's war effort, agreed to help Lenin return home. After travelling secretly through Germany and Sweden by train Lenin arrived at the Finland Station, Petrograd, in April 1917. Other leading Bolsheviks living in exile also hurried back to Russia.

The war with Germany continued. Food supplies ran short. Most Russians wanted peace. (D13) Lenin was against the war

Kerensky (at left) taking the salute at a military parade. He was a brilliant speaker but his Provisional Government failed to end the unpopular war or deal firmly with the Bolsheviks. Kerensky went to live in America where he became a professor of history

and in his speeches he used the popular demands of 'Bread, Peace, and Freedom'. Workers in the big industrial areas gave their support to the Bolsheviks who gained control of the Petrograd soviet. In July the Bolsheviks tried to take over the Government by force but the attempt failed. Then, in August, a general named Kornilov threatened to march on Petrograd with his troops and seize power. Kerensky, the leader of the Provisional Government, armed the workers of the Petrograd soviet. These 'Red Guards', as they were called, prepared to defend the city. However, Kornilov's soldiers deserted him and joined the workers. Many

The first 'Red' Guards with arms seized from the arsenals in Petrograd

more workers began to support the Bolsheviks because they feared that other generals might try to take over the government of Russia. The Bolsheviks in the capital grew steadily stronger. They were well organized and backed by armed workers, soldiers and sailors. Lenin decided that now was the time to try to take over the Government.

THE OCTOBER REVOLUTION

On the evening of 24th October the Bolshevik 'Red Guards' moved against the Provisional Government. They seized the bridges over the river Neva, occupied the main public buildings and the Winter Palace where the Provisional Government met. (D14) Within a few days the Bolsheviks controlled Petrograd, Moscow, and several other cities. (D15) Securing control of the whole of Russia, however, was to take much longer.

Why were the Bolsheviks able to seize power so easily? One reason was that the Provisional Government was very weak. It could not keep order in the countryside and the towns, or prevent soldiers deserting the army. The Bolsheviks were never a large group. In free elections held at the end of 1917 only a quarter of the people voted for them. But their supporters lived in the large industrial centres of the heart of Russia, and were disciplined, determined and united. Many of the Bolshevik leaders were ruthless men, like Lenin, who were prepared to do almost anything to gain and keep power. (D16)

Demonstrators fleeing from troops of the Provisional Government in Petrograd during the July riots 1917

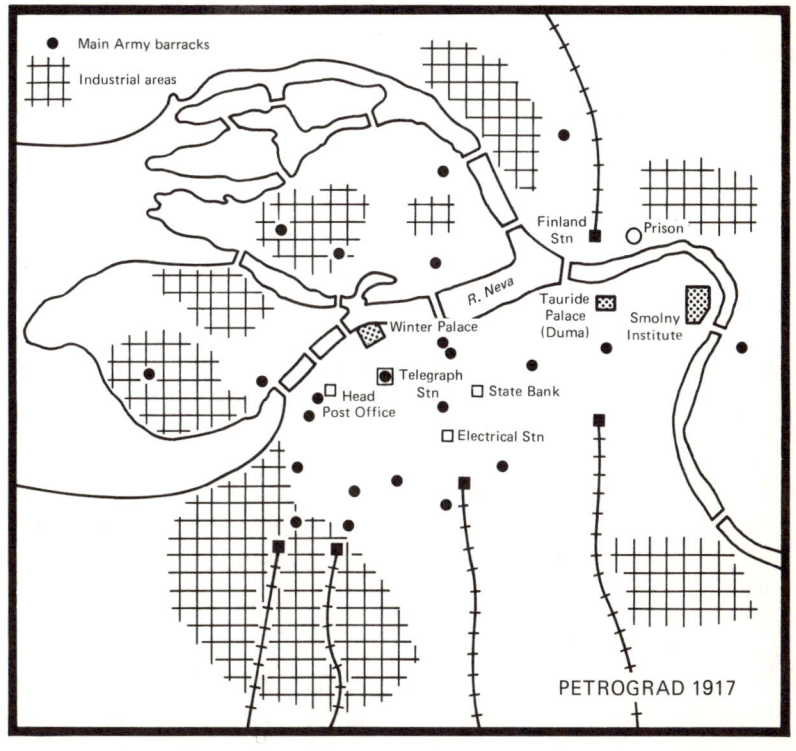

Petrograd, 1917

Lenin telling the Congress of Soviets to seize power, October 1917. A highly romantic view of the October Revolution painted by a Soviet artist after the death of Lenin. Notice that Josef Stalin, dictator of Russia, is given a prominent place behind Lenin

Although large parties opposed the Bolsheviks they were poorly organized and divided among themselves.

In the first months of Bolshevik control Lenin made a separate peace with Germany. A decree was passed giving the land to the peasants and all banks were taken over by the State. (D17) Lenin's aim was a Bolshevik, or Communist, dictatorship. He wasn't prepared to share power with other revolutionaries, or even fellow-Marxists, who didn't agree with his policies. Many of the anti-Bolsheviks prepared to fight Lenin's dictatorship.

THE CIVIL WAR

Before the war with Germany had ended civil war broke out in Russia. Several groups known as 'Whites' opposed the Bolsheviks. There were socialists, liberals, nationalists, and former Tsarist generals. They set up separate governments in different parts of Russia and began to fight the Bolsheviks. Britain and France supplied some of them with arms, and also sent soldiers, in the hope that if they won they would bring Russia back in to the war against Germany. In the east Japan, and in the west Poland, took advantage of the chaos caused by the civil war to seize large parts of Russian territory. Facing the Whites and the Poles was the Bolshevik Red Army. It was organized by Leon Trotsky, one of the most brilliant of the Soviet leaders.

For nearly three years the Reds and Whites fought each other all over Russia. (D18) The Bolsheviks won because they not only controlled the industrial areas but the Red Army was well trained and well led. The Whites lacked outstanding leaders, they were constantly divided, and at times even fought each other. France and Britain gave little help and soon withdrew from Russia.

Millions of people were killed in the fighting or died from starvation. During the war the Tsar and his family were killed by the Bolsheviks. The old Russian empire was gone for ever. But all the national groups were not free. When the revolution began many thought that they could break away from Russian rule and set up their own independent states. But gradually the Bolsheviks regained control of almost all the lands which had previously been ruled by the Tsar. The Bolsheviks now

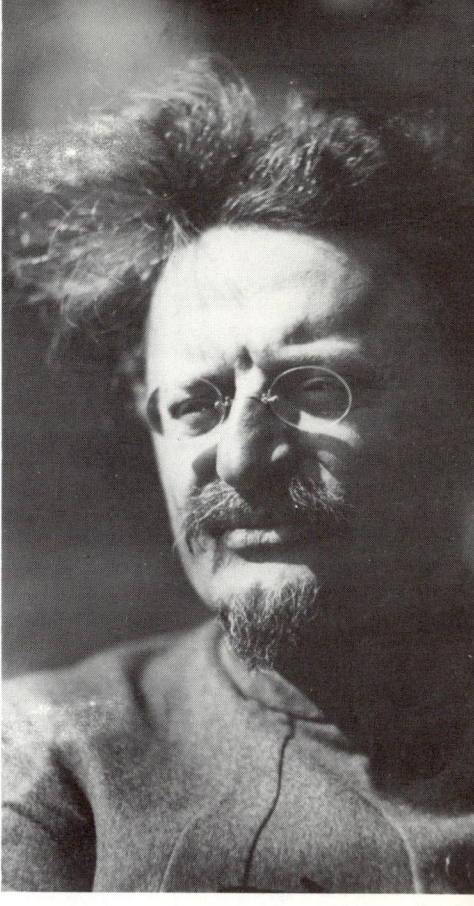

Leon Trotsky, the dynamic organizer of the Red Army. After Lenin's death Trotsky left Russia. He was murdered in 1940 on Stalin's orders

Students in Moscow drilling for the Red Army during the civil war

Red Guards storming the Winter Palace. From Eisenstein's film version of the October revolution Ten Days that Shook the World

called the new state the Union of Soviet Socialist Republics (USSR), or the Soviet Union. They hoped that as the Communist revolution spread other countries would join a union of socialist states. (D19)

THE CREATION OF THE SOVIET STATE

For Russia the civil war was an even greater disaster than the war with Germany had been. Much of the country was in ruins. Industries had been destroyed and everybody's way of life disrupted. Drastic measures were needed to restore order and to rebuild Russia's economy. Lenin and the Bolsheviks were quite prepared to use whatever methods were necessary. Secret police and firing squads got rid of people who dared to oppose them.

Lenin wanted to make Russia a Communist country with the State controlling industry and agriculture rather than leaving it in the hands of private individuals or companies. But even with the power he had at his disposal he was unable to change everything at once. The peasants, for example, would not easily give up the land that they had just seized for themselves. In 1921 Lenin introduced his 'New

Economic Policy' which allowed some private ownership to continue for a few more years. The State kept control of the important parts of the economy, such as railways, banks and large factories, while small workshops and farms were left in the hands of their owners.

The adoption of the 'New Economic Policy' was forced on Lenin by the desperate state of Russia's economy and the violent opposition of peasants, workers and soldiers. (D20, 21) This shows that the ideas and practice of Russian Communism do not always go together. Lenin was mainly interested in keeping power and transforming Russia. And to do this he was prepared to change his ideas if necessary. It was left to Stalin, Lenin's successor, to extend State ownership once Russia had fully recovered from the civil war.

But if economic changes came slowly, political and social changes came much more quickly. All power was placed in the hands of the Communist Party (the new name taken by the Bolsheviks) and other political organizations were banned. The power of the Orthodox Church was broken and the educational system was used to teach people to be good Communists. Russia was set on a new course for a new future.

The civil war and foreign intervention caused widespread destruction and famine throughout Russia. Hungry refugees at Samara, October 1921

THE EFFECTS OF THE REVOLUTION ON RUSSIA

The Revolution brought great and lasting changes to Russia. The Tsarist system of government was completely destroyed but the new Communist way of ruling Russia was similar in many ways. Under the old system the Tsar and his ministers had ruled as dictators. After 1917 Lenin and the leaders of the Communist Party became the dictators. Both the Tsarists and the Communists believed that there was one right way of looking at the world and that it was the duty of the Government to see that all Russians accepted it. The Tsar had used peoples' belief in the Orthodox Church to get obedience to his rule. The new Soviet Government educated people to accept the ideas of Marxism and forced them to obey the Communist Party.

Both before and after the revolution all important decisions about how Russia was ruled were made in the capital. Although Lenin had said that workers should control their own affairs through local soviets, in fact the Communist Party had much greater powers than the Tsar ever had. This was largely because Russia's industries continued to expand. Lenin wanted Russia to become a strong modern industrial state. As more people lived in towns and worked in factories, and as communications improved, it became easier for the government to enforce its control. Thousands of officials were used to do this. All newspapers and trade unions were run by the Communist Party, meetings were controlled, and the secret police killed and imprisoned opponents of the Government.

One of the most lasting changes brought about by the revolution was state control over industry. And for most people in Russia today, nearly sixty years after the revolution, a communist system of government and education is the only way of being ruled that they know.

THE RUSSIAN REVOLUTION AND WORLD REVOLUTION

Lenin thought that the First World War would lead to world revolution. It had caused so much suffering that the masses of ordinary people would want to follow the Bolshevik example. (D22) To further this aim Lenin founded the Communist International (Comintern) to encourage and co-ordinate the efforts of Communist parties in other countries. (D23) For a short time it seemed as though Lenin's dream might come true. Revolutionary republics calling themselves 'Soviets' were set up in southern Germany, Hungary and elsewhere. But they only lasted a few months. Established governments had little difficulty in keeping communist sympathizers under control. Most people in Europe had had enough of fighting. They would support existing governments so long as they kept order and gave them the chance of becoming better off.

With the failure of communist revolutions in Europe in 1921

Lenin gave up his attempts to link up directly with other Communist parties. The Comintern continued to exist but its new aim was to help communists in different countries gain control of trade unions and other political parties. They could then build up their strength ready to overthrow governments. This made many countries very suspicious of Russia. Some at first refused to trade with her and Russia did not join the League of Nations until 1934.

Stalin, who became dictator when Lenin died in 1924, said that Russian communists should think less about world revolution and concentrate on first building Russia into a strong socialist country. Russia's isolation was an important reason for the failure to establish a lasting peace after the First World War.

THE RUSSIAN REVOLUTION AND THE DEVELOPING WORLD

Karl Marx expected the communist revolution to start in those countries which had been first to industrialize – Britain, France, Germany, or the United States. But in fact it broke out in Russia, a country in which most people were peasant farmers and where industry was still being developed. Communists take their explanation for this from Lenin's book, *Imperialism, the Highest Stage of Capitalism*, which was written in 1916.

According to Lenin the capitalists in the industrial countries, in their search for even greater profits, were taking wealth from the poorer parts of the world. Thus, it was not simply a struggle of rich against poor *within* each nation but also a struggle between rich and poor nations. The poor nations were countries that could be used by the rich states for their own benefit. They were not only territories which had become European colonies but also weak states like China. In Lenin's view, Russia before 1917 had also been one of these exploited countries because Western capitalists owned shares in its railways and industries.

Lenin's ideas had a great deal of influence in Asia and Africa. To some nationalists they seemed to explain why their countries were poor. And Lenin's success in seizing power in Russia inspired them to think they could do the same in their own countries. (D24)

Communist ideas had great influence in China which had suffered for a century from the merchants and gunboats of the Western Powers. Inspired by Lenin's words and example Mao Tse-Tung led his Communist forces to complete victory in 1949 after more than twenty years of armed struggle. (*The Chinese Revolution*) With Chinese support communist governments also came to power in neighbouring North Vietnam and North Korea. Nowadays communist sympathizers in the developing countries of Asia, Africa and Latin America often look to China and the ideas of Mao Tse-Tung for inspiration, rather than to modern industrial Russia and the writings of Lenin.

DOCUMENT 1

PEASANT CONDITIONS   *From a police report, 1905*

Very often the peasants do not have enough allotment land, and cannot during the year feed themselves, clothe themselves, heat their homes, keep their tools and livestock, secure seed for sowing and, lastly discharge all their taxes and obligations, to the state, the zemstvo [local assemblies] and the commune.

DOCUMENT 2

THE COMMUNIST MANIFESTO, 1848   *KARL MARX*

The history of all hitherto existing society is the history of class struggles. Freeman and slave, patrician and plebian, lord and serf, guild-master and journeyman, in a word, oppressor and oppressed, stood in constant opposition to one another, carried on an uninterrupted, now hidden, now open fight, a fight that each time ended, either in a revolutionary reconstitution of society at large, or in the common ruin of the contending classes.... The development of modern industry, therefore, cuts from under the feet of the bourgeoisie [capitalists] the very foundation on which [they] produce and appropriate products. Its fall and the victory of the proletariat [workers] are equally inevitable....

The immediate aim of the Communists is the ... formation of the proletariat into a class, overthrow of the bourgeois supremacy, conquest of political power.... The theory of the Communists may be summed up in the single sentence: Abolition of private property....

The proletariat will use its political supremacy to wrest all capital from the bourgeoisie, to centralize all instruments of production in the hands of the state.... Communists everywhere support every revolutionary movement against the existing social and political order.... They openly declare that their ends can only be attained by the forcible overthrow of all existing social conditions. Let the ruling class tremble at a communist revolution. The proletarians have nothing to lose but their chains. They have a world to win. Working men of all countries, unite!

DOCUMENT 3

BOLSHEVIK ORGANIZATION *LENIN – In 1902 he described how a revolutionary party should be organized.*

... there can be no revolutionary movement without a revolutionary theory... the role of the vanguard fighter can be fulfilled only by a party which is guided by Marxist theory.... The most revolutionary of all the immediate tasks that confront the workers is the destruction of the most powerful bulwark of European and Asiatic reaction – the Russian government. The direct practical leadership of the movement can only be exercised by a special central group which includes all the best revolutionary forces from among the Russian Social-Democrats and is in charge of all the work relevant to the whole of the party, such as the distribution of literature, the publishing of leaflets, the distribution of forces, the appointment of persons and groups to manage special undertakings, the preparation of all-Russian demonstrations and of insurrection.... An organization of revolutionaries must embrace first of all and chiefly people whose profession consists of revolutionary activity. In the face of this common feature any distinction between workers and intellectuals must be completely obliterated.

DOCUMENT 4

'BLOODY SUNDAY' *A peaceful crowd of 200,000, led by Father Gapon, an Orthodox priest, marched to the Winter Palace in Petrograd to appeal directly to the Tsar to improve living conditions. This is part of their petition.*

Lord. We workers, our children, our wives and our old, helpless parents have come, Lord, to seek truth and protection from you. We are impoverished and oppressed, unbearable work is imposed on us, we are despised and not recognized as human beings. We are treated as slaves, who must bear their fate and be silent. We have suffered terrible things, but we are pressed ever deeper into the abyss of poverty, ignorance and lack of rights. Despotism and arbitrariness throttle us and we choke. We have no more strength, O Lord. The limit of patience is here; for us that terrible moment has come when death is better than the continuance of the most unbearable torments.

DOCUMENT 5

THE MASSACRE   FATHER GAPON – *Describing how hundreds of people were killed on 'Bloody Sunday'*

The procession moved in a compact mass. At last we reached within two hundred paces of where the troops stood. Files of infantry barred the road, and in front of them a company of Cossack cavalry with their drawn swords shining in the sun. Would they dare to touch us? Suddenly the Cossacks galloped towards us. A cry of alarm arose as they came down on us. I saw the swords lifted and falling, the men, women, and children dropping to the earth like logs of wood, while moans, curses, and shouts filled the air. Again we started forward, with rising rage in our hearts. The Cossacks turned their horses and began to cut their way through the crowd from the rear. We were still advancing when suddenly, without any warning, was heard the dry crack of many rifle-shots. I turned rapidly to the crowd and shouted to them to lie down. As we lay thus another volley was fired, and another, and yet another, till it seemed as though the firing was continuous. At last the firing ceased. Bodies lay prostrate around me. I cried to them, 'Stand up!'. But they lay still, their arms stretched out lifelessly, and the scarlet stain of blood upon the snow. Horror crept into my heart. The thought flashed through my mind. 'And this is the work of our Little Father, the Tsar.' 'There is no longer any Tsar for us!' I exclaimed.

DOCUMENT 6

RUSSIA'S FIRST CONSTITUTION   TSAR NICHOLAS II – *Explaining to his mother his decision to grant a constitution*

You remember, no doubt, those January days when we were together at Tsarskoe – they were miserable, weren't they? But they are *nothing* in comparison with what has happened now. All sorts of conferences took place in Moscow; God knows what happened in the universities. Every *kind* of riffraff walked in from the streets, riot was loudly proclaimed – nobody seemed to mind. It makes me sick to read the news! ... But the Ministers, instead of acting with quick decision, only assemble in council like a lot of frightened hens and cackle about providing united ministerial action. One had the same feeling as before a thunderstorm in summer! ... There were only two ways open; to find an energetic soldier and crush the rebellion by sheer force. That would mean rivers of blood, and in the end we should be where we had started. The other way out would be to give to the people their civil rights, freedom of speech and press, also to have all laws confirmed by a State Duma – that, of course, would be a constitution.... We discussed it for two days and in the end, invoking God's help, I signed. In my telegram I could not explain all the circumstances which brought me to this terrible decision, which nevertheless I took quite consciously.... There was no other way out than to cross oneself and give what everyone was asking for.

DOCUMENT 7

THE EFFECTS OF THE WAR KRIVOSHEIN – *The Minister of Agriculture describes the consequences of the defeats of 1915.*

Hungry and destitute people are bringing panic everywhere, and extinguish all the vestiges of the enthusiasm of the first months of the war. [Refugees] move in a solid mass, they tread down the fields, destroy the meadows and woods.... The railway lines are congested; even movements of military trains and shipments of food will soon become impossible. I do not know what is going on in the areas that fall into the hands of the enemy, but I do know that not only the immediate rear of our army but the remote rear as well are devastated, ruined.

DOCUMENT 8

A WARNING TO THE TSAR MICHAEL RODZIANKO – *The outspoken President of the State Duma, reporting to Tsar Nicholas, 20th January 1917*

Your Majesty was able to gather from my second report that I consider the state of the country to have become more critical and menacing than ever. The spirit of the people is such that the gravest upheavals may be expected.... All Russia is unanimous in claiming a change of Government ... invested with the confidence of the nation.... To our shame chaos reigns everywhere. There is no Government and no system.... At every turn one is confronted with abuses and confusion. The nation realizes that you banished from the Government all those in whom the Duma and the people trusted, and replaced them by unworthy and incompetent men.... No wonder monstrous rumours are afloat of treason and espionage in the rear of the army. Sire, there is not a single honest or reliable man left in your entourage: all the best have either been eliminated or resigned.

'Give me facts', said the Emperor, 'there are no facts to confirm your statements.'

'Your Majesty, do not compel the people to choose between you and the good of the country.'

The Emperor pressed his head between his hands, then said: 'Is it possible that for twenty-two years I have tried to act for the best, and that for twenty-two years it was all a mistake?'

It was a hard moment. With a great effort at self-control I replied: 'Yes, your Majesty, for twenty-two years you have followed a wrong course.'

DOCUMENT 9

OUTBREAK OF REVOLUTION   *MAURICE PALEOLOGUE – The French Ambassador recalling in his diary, 1917*

Thursday, February 23: In Petrograd all day processions have been parading the main streets. At several points the mob shouted for 'Bread and peace!'.

Friday, February 24: This morning the excitement in industrial circles took a violent form. Many bakeries were looted. At several points the Cossacks charged the crowd and killed a number of workmen.

Monday, February 27: The Volhynian regiment mutinied during the night, killed its officers and was parading the city, calling on the people to take part in the revolution and trying to win over troops who still remain loyal. . . . I went out to see what was happening. Frightened inhabitants were scattering through the streets. Soldiers were helping civilians to erect barricades. Flames mounted from the Law Courts. The gates of the arsenal burst open with a crash. Suddenly the crack of machine-gun fire split the air; it was the regulars who had just taken up position near the Nevsky Prospect. The revolutionaries replied. Fighting was in progress in every part of the city.

DOCUMENT 10

TELEGRAM TO TSAR NICHOLAS, 27th FEBRUARY 1917
MICHAEL RODZIANKO

The last bulwark of order has been removed. The Government is completely powerless to suppress disorder. The troops of the garrison are unreliable. The reserve battalions of the Guard regiments are caught up by the revolt. They kill their officers. Joining the mob and the popular movement they advance to the building of the Ministry of Internal Affairs and to the State Duma. Civil war has begun and blazes up. Give orders immediately to summon a new government which will enjoy public confidence. . . . Do not delay, Sire. If the movement spreads to the army the fall of the dynasty is inevitable.

DOCUMENT 11

THE ABDICATION OF NICHOLAS II

In the days of the great struggle against the foreign enemies, who for nearly three years have tried to enslave our fatherland, the Lord God has been pleased to send down on Russia a new heavy trial. Internal popular disturbances threaten to have a disastrous effect on the future conduct of this persistent war. The destiny of Russia, the honour of our heroic army, the welfare of the people and the whole future of our dear fatherland demand that the war should be brought to a victorious conclusion whatever the cost. The cruel enemy is making his last efforts, and already the hour approaches when our glorious army together with our gallant allies will crush him. In these decisive days in the life of Russia, We thought it Our duty of conscience to facilitate for Our people the closest union possible and a consolidation of all national forces for the speedy attainment of victory. In agreement with the Imperial Duma We have thought it well to renounce the Throne of the Russian Empire and to lay down the supreme power.

DOCUMENT 12

THE PEASANTS SEIZE THE LAND   *A report to the Provisional Government from Kyazan Province, mid-1917*

. . . The character of the destruction is now different from what it was in 1905-6. Then the peasants did not in general prevent the landlords from removing their possessions — furniture, crockery, silver, household goods and so forth. Now the picture has changed. The possessions of the landlords are removed to the last item and distributed per head of family. It cannot be said that the peasants as a whole take part in these depredations. Often the village assembly decides, before the destruction, to keep the landlord's house for peasant use – as a school, for example – but words and actions differ and so the movement of the peasants towards the estate generally ends with incendiarism and destruction. There are rarely acts of violence of any sort against those living in the manor houses. Only some cases of beatings by the crowd are to be noted.

DOCUMENT 13

MORALE AT THE FRONT   *An official report, September 1917*

... because of general war-weariness, bad nourishment, mistrust of officers, etc., there has developed an intense defeatist agitation accompanied by refusals to carry out orders, threats to the commanding personnel, and attempts to fraternize with Germans. Everywhere one hears voices calling for immediate peace, because, they say, no one will stay in the trenches during the winter.

DOCUMENT 14

THE BOLSHEVIK COUP   *JOHN REED – An American friend of Lenin who was in Petrograd when the Bolsheviks seized power*

Towards four in the morning I met Zorin in the outer hall, a rifle slung from his shoulder.

'We're moving!' said he, calmly, but with satisfaction. 'We pinched the Assistant Minister of Justice and the Minister of Religions. They're down the cellar now. One regiment is on the march to capture the Telephone Exchange, another the Telegraph Agency, another the State Bank. The Red Guard is out. . . .'

On the steps of the Smolny Institute [Lenin's headquarters], in the chill dark, we first saw the Red Guard – a huddled group of boys in workmen's clothes, carrying guns with bayonets, talking nervously together.

Far over the still roofs westward came the sound of scattered rifle fire, where the Government troops were trying to open the bridges over the Neva, to prevent the factory workers and soldiers of the Viborg quarter from joining the Soviet forces in the centre of the city; and the Kronstadt sailors were closing them again... Wednesday, 25th October, I rose very late. It was a raw, chill day. In front of the State Bank some soldiers with fixed bayonets were standing at the closed gates.

'What side do you belong to?', I asked. 'The Government?'
'No more Government,' one answered with a grin. '*Slava Bogu!* Glory to God!'

DOCUMENT 15

END OF THE PROVISIONAL GOVERNMENT *NIKOLAY SUKHANOV — One of the revolutionaries describes the final defeat of the Provisional Government*

During the whole of the 28th [October] very disquieting news of Kerensky's offensive continued to be received. The Bolsheviks took feverish action. From morning till night troops, mostly Red Army men, were being moved to the front. Masses of workers were sent outside the town to dig trenches. Petrograd was festooned with barbed-wire entanglements. On the 30th it was decided to finish Kerensky at one blow. The Kronstadt and Helsingfors sailors detachments were moved *en bloc* to the front. Trotsky himself went too; from now on he was invariably to be present at the most critical points all over the country. And by the end of that night Trotsky was already reporting to Petrograd from Pulkov: 'KERENSKY IS IN RETREAT – we are advancing...'

The liquidation of Kerensky completed the October Revolution. Moscow was still an arena of bitter struggle, and the enemies of the Bolsheviks were still far from laying down their arms. Now, however, there was in the Smolny Institute a unified and indivisible Government of the Republic, and its enemies had become rebels and nothing more. The revolution that had placed a workers party at the head of a first-class world Power was accomplished. A new chapter had opened in the working-class movement of the world and in the history of the Russian State.

DOCUMENT 16

THE USE OF TERROR *TROTSKY — Writing in 1920 about the Civil War in his book* Terrorism and Communism

The working class, which seized power in battle, had as its object and its duty to establish that power unshakeably, to guarantee its own supremacy beyond question, to destroy its enemies, and thereby to make sure of carrying out Socialist reforms. Otherwise there would be no point in seizing power. The revolution does demand of the revolutionary class that it should attain its end by all methods at its disposal — if necessary, by an armed rising; if required, by terrorism. A revolutionary class which has conquered power with arms in its hands is bound to, and will, suppress, rifle in hand, all attempts to tear the power out of its hand.

The question of the form of repression, or of its degree, of course, is not one of 'principle'. It is a question of expediency.

DOCUMENT 17

PROCLAMATION BY THE CONGRESS OF SOVIETS, 27 OCTOBER 1917

Supported by an overwhelming majority of the workers, soldiers, and peasants, and basing itself on the victorious insurrection of the workers and the garrison of Petrograd, the Congress hereby resolves to take governmental power into its own hands.

The Provisional Government is deposed and most of its members are under arrest.

The Soviet authority will at once propose a democratic peace to all nations and an immediate armistice on all fronts. It will safeguard the transfer without compensation of all land to the peasant committees; it will defend the soldiers' rights, introducing complete democratization of the army, it will establish workers' control over industry, it will insure the convocation of the Constituent Assembly on the date set, it will supply the cities with bread and the villages with articles of first necessity, and it will secure to all nationalities inhabiting Russia the right of self-determination.

The Congress resolves that all local authority shall be transferred to the Soviets of Workers', Soldiers', and Peasants' Deputies, which are charged with the task of enforcing revolutionary order.

The Congress calls upon the soldiers in the trenches to be watchful and steadfast. The Congress of Soviets is confident that the revolutionary army will know how to defend the revolution against all imperialistic attempts until the new government has concluded a democratic peace which it is proposing directly to all nations.

DOCUMENT 18

THE PROGRESS OF THE REVOLUTION   *A British businessman writing in 1918*

In the villages the peasant will not give grain to the Bolsheviks because he hates them. Armed companies are sent out everywhere from Petrograd and Moscow to take the grain from the peasant, and every day all over Russia fights for grain are fought to a finish. . . . In the Red Army for any military offence there is only one punishment — death. If a regiment retreats against orders machine-guns are turned on them, and if the commissar of the regiment cannot thus hold his men he is shot. . . . The position of the bourgeoisie defies all description. . . . Payments by the banks have been stopped. It is forbidden to sell furniture or to move it from one house to another. All owners and managers of works, offices and shops have been called up for compulsory labour. . . . In Petrograd . . . hundreds of people are dying weekly from hunger. . . . The political parties most oppressed by the Bolsheviks are the Socialists, Social Democrats [Marxists], and Social Revolutionaries. Many members who have worked all their time for the revolution, have been arrested or shot. . . . The Bolsheviks continue to hold power by a system of terrorism and tyranny. People are arrested every day in hundreds, and kept in prison months without any trial. Bolshevism in Russia offers to our civilization a menace and until it is ruthlessly destroyed we may expect trouble, strikes, revolutions everywhere.

DOCUMENT 19

A COMMUNIST WORLD FEDERATION *In April 1918 the Bolsheviks drafted a constitution for the new Soviet Union. This is the opinion of one speaker in the debate.*

Our constitution is of world-wide significance. As the workers and peasants from different countries take advantage of favourable circumstances and follow the example of Soviet Russia, the Russian Soviet republic sooner or later will be surrounded by daughter and sister republics, which united will lay the basis for a federation first of Europe and then of the entire world.

DOCUMENT 20

THE NEW ECONOMIC POLICY *LENIN — An explanation (in 1921) of why the Soviet Government had to change its economic policies*

Our poverty and ruin are so great that we cannot at one stroke restore large-scale factory state socialist production. This requires that we accumulate large stocks of grains and fuels in the big industrial centres, replace worn-out machines with new ones, and so on. Experience has convinced us that this cannot be done at one stroke.... We must try to satisfy the demands of the peasants who are dissatisfied, discontented, and cannot be otherwise.... In essence the small farmer can be satisfied with two things. First of all, there must be a certain amount of freedom of trade, of freedom for the small private owner; and, secondly, commodities and products must be provided.

DOCUMENT 21

THE KRONSTADT REVOLT   *Harsh Bolshevik rule caused workers, soldiers and the sailors at the naval base at Kronstadt, near Petrograd, to revolt in February 1921.*

A complete change is necessary in the policies of the Government. First of all, the workers and peasants need freedom. They don't want to live by the decrees of the Bolsheviks; they want to control their own destinies. Comrades, preserve revolutionary order! Determinedly and in an organized manner demand: Liberation of all arrested Socialists and non-partisan working-men; abolition of martial law; freedom of speech, press, and assembly for all who labour.

DOCUMENT 22

THE WORLD SIGNIFICANCE OF THE OCTOBER REVOLUTION
JOSEPH STALIN — The Bolshevik People's Commissar for Nationalities, writing in the Communist paper Pravda, *November 1918*

The October revolution is the first revolution in the history of the world to break the age-long sleep of the toiling masses of the oppressed peoples of the east and to draw them into the fight against world imperialism.
   The great world significance of the October revolution is, primarily, that it has — by this very fact built a bridge between the socialist west and the enslaved east, creating a new revolutionary front, which runs from the workers of the west through the Russian revolution to the oppressed peoples of the east, against world imperialism.

DOCUMENT 23

THE COMMUNIST INTERNATIONAL

PROCLAMATION 1919
'Proletarians of all lands! In the war against imperialistic barbarity, against monarchy, against the privileged classes, against the bourgeois state and bourgeois property, against all forms and varieties of . . . oppression – UNITE!

PROCLAMATION 1920
'The Communist International has proclaimed the cause of Soviet Russia as its own . . . Working men and women! On this earth there is only one banner which is worth fighting and dying for. It is the banner of the Communist International!'

DOCUMENT 24

MODEL FOR REVOLUTION *Sun Yat-sen's widow calls on the Chinese to follow the Bolshevik example, 1927*

I call upon all men and women, the youth of China, and especially the workers, peasants, students and volunteers, to unite and organize this struggle for the liberation, unity and integrity of China, a struggle inseparably bound up with the efforts for the emancipation of the toiling masses from exploitation, with the fight for the rights of free speech, free press, assembly and organization, and for the liberation of political prisoners. . . . Let us remember that the Soviet Revolution demonstrated the superiority of a revolutionary people and its revolutionary armies over the forces of the whole capitalist world. The Chinese people with its already great revolutionary tradition will conquer in the same way. Not imperialist domination and the dismemberment of China, but a free, united revolutionary China of the workers and peasants!

ACKNOWLEDGMENTS

Illustrations

Contemporary Films pages 7 top, 16; The Mansell Collection pages 4 (both pictures), 5, 9, 13, 14; The Radio Times Hulton Picture Library pages 3, 6, 7 bottom, 8, 10, 11, 12, 15 both pictures, 17.

Documents

D1, 3, 4, 7, 8, *Russia in Revolution,* Lionel Kocham, George Weidenfeld and Nicolson; D9, *The Bolshevik Revolution 1917-1918,* Bunyan and Fisher, Stanford University Press; D10, *The Russian Revolution, Vol. I,* W. H. Chamberlin, Macmillan Publishing Co., New York; D14, *Ten Days That Shook The World,* John Reed, Lawrence & Wishart Ltd; D19, *Why Lenin? Why Stalin?,* T. H. von Laue, George Weidenfeld and Nicolson.

Greenhaven World History Program

History Makers
Alexander
Constantine
Leonardo Da Vinci
Columbus
Luther, Erasmus and Loyola
Napoleon
Bolivar
Adam Smith, Malthus and Marx
Darwin
Bismark
Henry Ford
Roosevelt
Stalin
Mao Tse-Tung
Gandhi
Nyerere and Nkrumah

Great Civilizations
The Ancient Near East
Ancient Greece
Pax Romana
The Middle Ages
Spices and Civilization
Chingis Khan and the Mongol Empire
Akbar and the Mughal Empire
Traditional China
Ancient America
Traditional Africa
Asoka and Indian Civilization
Mohammad and the Arab Empire
Ibin Sina and the Muslim World
Suleyman and the Ottoman Empire

Great Revolutions
The Neolithic Revolution
The Agricultural Revolution
The Scientific Revolution
The Industrial Revolution
The Communications Revolution
The American Revolution
The French Revolution
The Mexican Revolution
The Russian Revolution
The Chinese Revolution

Enduring Issues
Cities
Population
Health and Wealth
A World Economy
Law
Religion
Language
Education
The Family

Political and Social Movements
The Slave Trade
The Enlightenment
Imperialism
Nationalism
The British Raj and Indian Nationalism
The Growth of the State
The Suez Canal
The American Frontier
Japan's Modernization
Hitler's Reich
The Two World Wars
The Atom Bomb
The Cold War
The Wealth of Japan
Hollywood